Misuse
Julia Rose Lewis

Newton-le-Willows

Published in the United Kingdom in 2024
by The Knives Forks And Spoons Press,
51 Pipit Avenue,
Newton-le-Willows,
Merseyside,
WA12 9RG.

ISBN 978-1-916590-05-2

Copyright © Julia Rose Lewis 2024.

The right of Julia Rose Lewis to be identified as the author of this work has been asserted by them in accordance with the Copyrights, Designs and Patents Act of 1988. All rights reserved. No part of this publication may be reproduced, stored in a retrieval system, transmitted in any form or by any means, electronic, photocopying, recording or otherwise, without prior permission of the publisher.

Acknowledgements:

Poems from 'No Ordinary Work' were published as a pamphlet by The Storybox Collective.

'alcea rosea' and 'in a hospital light' were published by *Sand Journal*.

'I am visual hapticity' was exhibited at Writing Cultures Para-ability: An Exhibition 2023 at The Dean's Space, Knights Park Kingston University.

In addition, special thanks are due to those who generously contributed to the GoFundMe campaign to assist in the costs of the production of this collection.

Contents

Green Day   5

Tourmaline   17

No Ordinary Work   45

Millionth Then   75

The Man Trap   91

Sordes   97

Green Day

green log

Unentitled

ear reciprocal
there there verdigris says gray as yesterday
if finding the filmouse in the field
here is wholesome to muses

Julia Rose Lewis

Mouseas

verdigris
verdigris
grey overrunning green
green overrunning grey
to be obsolete leap to loop to bound dinosaur
inside grief finds gregarious us standing as grass sees
we might be touching feeling and feeling green
as verdigris dyer reseda

The Green Market

loop is also close
to enclose
lasso in this way the wall is wallowing lift
a winding line inside a window
so often
he is as grass sensuality
a feeling greening is living reverse sand
find me in london
in touch with material-affective dimensions
connect eye we talk cut to willing company green yarn
in mint condition
touch is but an electromagnetic interaction
where fingers come into green
they are always sensing the electromagnetic repulsion
between the electrons in their fingers and in the grass
they repel one another
even in willing company
green is but an electromagnetic interaction
it is grease stains
gross says what about the battle ropes?

for the love of green skeins held under gray skies
and pushing the tale physics utilizes
he asks me what three shots of espresso in a coffee is called
and I tell him a green eye because the jealous sea
is willing to tell itself about touching repulsion
is pulling
is he writing about the green keep?

Julia Rose Lewis

Waiting for a Field Mouse

green
inspired down
to be obsolete leap to loop
the blue tulip will lift
for the love of elevating indeterminate touching
if and only if feigning grain inside grass

grass
is only feeling green
noise inside crows and crochet touching
books and flies to be binding to be found down
hooks and eyes and skies and lift
until left behind another loop

loop
is also close to enclose grass
lasso in this way the wall is wallowing lift
life is finding many ways to behead green
to be holding down
to add devotion to indeterminate touch

touch
chooses to say it stays chasing a tulip loop
instead down
it finds itself a dirty grass-
hopper read dark gray is green
again negative is never pure or innocent lift

lift
left feeling touching
is gross oh hand over handy yellow waiting on green
is loping along the lollipop loop
is also obsolete woodlouse sitting in the grass
is mouse sitting himself filed down

Misuse

down
is told telling collecting shells and sea glass to feel lift
inside grief finds gregarious us standing as grass
to feeling touch
yearning over verdigris yarn fastened into a loop
it is touching green

it is touching feeling itself filed down
fastened it is the end loop if and only if lift
the atmosphere here is also green beheading grass

Julia Rose Lewis

Green Nomenclature:
Adapted from Werner's Nomenclature of Colors

is asparagus green?
is pistachio mixed with much grey wishes white?

as so happens sap
is an underside of lower wings of orange tip butterfly
is upper disk of leaves of woody night shade

if and only if foliage of lignum vitae
is olive green
is grass green mixed with much brown in wood dense

be little beetles scaraboeus as seen nobilis
is grass green
is emerald mixed with a little lemonade

emerald is as
emerald does
is a beauty spot on a wing of a teal drake

animal and shell of common water snail
is oil green
is emerald mixed with lemonade and chestnut
and yellow wishes grey low maintenance pets

apple as a foal
is an underside of wings of a green-brown moth
is emerald mixed with a little grey wishes white
is chrysoprase
is silica and a nickel little

Misuse

a winding line inside a window
is serpentine
is black wishes green
is grass mixed with a considerable portion of black

a green afterwards
or green wishes blue in the action
of dilute acetic acid on thin copper plates

is growing verdigris
is a tail of a small long-tailed green parrot to copper green feelings

is silver-leaved almond
is mountain green is
composed of emerald with much blue and a little yellow wishes grey

a hurricane neck of eider drake
is pistachio green
is emerald mixed with a lemonade
and a quantity of brown as seen in eider down

a little will dine on celindine green
is composed of verdigris and ashes to ashes we all fall down

Julia Rose Lewis

battle ropes:
after sj fowler

beside me mouse
is watching a recoding of sand
doing what it was inspired to do with battle ropes
with green
with eel grass with the verdigris
and ash should give it is celandine all the way down
it is tuesday all the way down
mouse
is a fulfilling louse in love with verdigris
is singing to the grey pilothouse door inside outside sand
a third demands green
in name in the obsolete sense bird internet trip ropes
rosa rugosa goes hips over ropes
close as self filed down
in the obsolete sense an unhealed wound turns green
or pasture grass sensuous mouse
soft focus on sand
on a tail of a small long-tailed parrot is the definition of verdigris
ring around the rosa rugosa singing verdigris
pocket full of ropes
sand
ashes to ashore to ashes we all fall down
we all find a field mouse
in the obsolete sense unhealed would be green
is saying grain on grey on green
verdigris
is saying amber grey muse is saying tu m'amuse is saying mouse
ropes sing to reap and hope
it is silver glowing grey all the way down
it is living reverse sand
it is sand
it is grey on neon flowering pink and green

down
singing verdigris
pretend it is a city a pasture rope
it is complicated feeding a quantum mouse
verdigris sand
ringing around the ropes saying he is too damn green
now it is complicated with the field mouse all the way down

Tourmaline

---
mined from on touching – the inhuman that therefore I am
my own muse's favorite color is green

Tourmaline

touch
is a grass sensuality
a feeling – greening on pressure presence proximity
close as one self filed down to hands
to enliven
uncanny grass senses of the self filed down
a literal holding of the self filed distance
in the grass sensation
in the greeting within the green
within the touch is an infinity of mice

a green close is the measure of closeness
if infectious diseases do not
if a measured reading does answer to make
the hair of nearly everyone stand on end
I can green
on even a few aspects of touch
offer what it might mean to come to infinite finitude
here in the interstices
it is reiterative lively stories all the way down
is diffractively threaded through
and enfolded
is that not the nature of touching?
is that not the nature of green negatives?
is touching not by its very nature all the ways an involution and
invitation and invisitation and wanted?

Julia Rose Lewis

I am visual hapticity
and grass sense
and horses signaling pretend it's a city
and the force of touching feeling
and dance
and green entanglement
it is just a few grasses sensuous
a few figurations in some serious play
itself filed down
for all the varied diary entries
focus says it is a richly inventive endeavor for the world
and second it distinguishes itself filed down inside
it is not above
it is not outside science
no less than laboratory workers modelers technicians and
technology to be grounded
if rigorous is when a bench is without the illusion of clean hands
inside and outside the world

there is a form experimenting in green
it is only alive
keeping patters and murmurs ringing walls

here is requiring aliveness
allowing oneself filed down and lured and surprised
it is not mere pronouncements
there are living recon figures ringing the world
the world there experiments with itself filed down
for the love of figure rings and recon figurines
inanimate
it does not merely embody math there
the weather is not only an unfolding algorithm
life is given in molecules
jellyfish coral reefs
rocks are material matters
brittle stars asteroids
and icebergs testing the waterbed
then snowflakes making leaps here or there
or rather testing the water yet
making here and there from leap year patterns
might be thought experiments
to be have been could still have been coral
it is shifting the familial corral

it is actively void
it bounds off the beaten path
then green touching down again going out
as swerving moves experiments in indeterminacy
spinning in green
in old directions it loses ideas
if a love affair with all life forms of liveliness is research
then to be green
is to be touching response and ability

Julia Rose Lewis

touching feelings is physics
its entire history is articulating touch
what touch
what green entails
when particles sense one another green
it is first contact with a mermaid named diethyl ether either
green action at a distance forces
seaweed fields
and exchange of virtual particles
will direct contact to touch green
or diethyl ether or action at a distance forces
or seaweed fields for the exchange of virtual particles calls out
how what how what how
what what how how what how
what once the exchange of energy entails
is motion effected down is temperature is pressing sure

does the eye seesaw
to the waterbed
to the emotion effected the figurehead?
does the eye see diethyl ether?
does the mind remember ethyl merman?
does the eye see in green lenses
the kinds of forces that particles call experience?
many kinds is the nature of measurement
in this way dizzying things shift
to touching feeling a love affair with history
a torquing
a perturbation a fair description
a way to opening green nature for physics and touch

tourmaline on the main line
in touch with material-affective dimensions
straying while staying alive
in green
in touch in the remainder
did itself engaging straying staying active
in touch
in green
all while touch is physicality virtuality affectivity emotional
locality
whereby being green in pretend touching feeling
always leaves the affective falls scientific

green is but an electromagnetic interaction
touch is but an electromagnetic interaction

an explanation for the physics of green
is that it does not involve touching feeling
an explanation for the physics of touching feeling
is green not
yes is no to touching feeling
you may think you are touching green when you raise
grass to your mouth
your hand is not touching the grass
sure you can finger the grass surface
it is exterior right
where your fingers come into green
you are always sensing the electromagnetic repulsion
between the electrons in your fingers and in the grass
they repel one another
and you decrease the distance between
then the repulsive force increases because
you cannot embarrass two electrons into green near to each other

Julia Rose Lewis

the reason feels or the feels
or even hands have effected all we ever feel
is the electromagnetic we seek
is mostly empty
is more or less an atom hinting at its perimeter bear
is not first contact forever repulsion
sells negative lives
to particles calling and pushing the tale physics utilizes
to tell itself about touching repulsion
green repulsion when green attraction had had enough

quantum touching is the feeling
growing these queer radishes as we wish

the field allows radishes
to grow new in existence no longer lives
(eternity dies) and there is a radish deconstructing identity
in ways even found
the field will bellow a call that alluring murmur wall wall
insensible the radishes growing to rework
the field is philosophical all the way down to nurture
a rugged and unexplored and emerald terrain
no way around unfortunate lately
only a light touch
grazing green
not sufficient time to give a rich sense of earth science

the field differs in its formalism in its ontology
it inherits the ontology only particles and void
and newly added fields

once upon a time particle fields and the void distant class
to things whereas
they are intra-related things in the field
to take one instance to field
it is particles called quanta of the field
that is the quantum of the electromagnetic field is a photograph
the quantum of a gravitational field is a gravestone
the quantum of an electric fence
will find itself in a field of electrons
and so onwards walking into another fear for the future
for the landscape happens to be the relationship
between particles and the void
could continue to make relationships to inspire radishes
or regard wishes for now
falling low that to note that pace
that particles no longer take their place in the void
nay rather they are entangled
with the void no longer vacuous
it is living indeterminacy
in the stead of vacuum of virtuality of the virtual particles
it is not rapid stupidity
it is not despite the tale telling that particles go in and out
of the vacuum faster than their existence
can be detected
hay rather indeterminacy
is having a field day performing experiments
inside virtuality is a kind of thought experiment
the world performs

virtual particles do not travel in traffic
they do not pretend to exist
in the present tense
it is only ghostly non existences that teeter on virtuality
itself an infinitely fine blade of grass
for the love of virtual particles is very difficult to grasp
it is quantized indeterminacies-in-action
the vacuum as somewhere for the love of wild activities ...

the field is not difficult to find
trouble is not double trouble is not trouble
it is around every corner
it inhabits us
it rabbits us turns round and round
so we inhabit it we have habits
we ribbit it or rather everything and nothing and the void

the field understands the green nature of the election
or rather other
parts turn out even and devoid
and even the particle the point particle likes the election
to cause all kinds of difficulties for the field
to be fair in the very fever the evidence
there is the field itself

in the nineteenth then the election
to be to have been a tiny sphere however tiny
a sphere a ball a bit
with bits of green negative covering the surface
with bits of green negative distributed
over remembering
and liking that you remember
and repel the green negatives themselves from themselves
see my muse is all the bits of green negatives
they repel
they repulse themselves on the surface of the sphere
they repulse the sphere all the way
there is no positive vibe unlikely to mitigate the repulsion
to navigate the repulsion
each bit feels the self repulsion
is self revulsion
the election has own self energy and would be too much to bear
itself filed down
it issues the green need to better understand

the election is a green negative
it is a point
it is a particle calling it is what
it is what it is this way eliminated difficulty
called self-revulsion
also called self-repulsion
it is bits because it eliminated bits here and there
it is just a point to carry a green negative
then the radio also is
then and therefore no radius
then and therefore self repulsion pushes
a green new infinity for the particle is interacting with the field
the field is infinite
it is a fox it is a paradox it is believed
to be resolved by the field

infinities persisted in the field
if the infinities mean dandelion greens
then they multiplied
when pulled
the field tried to resolve the dandelions
self-interaction until it felt less repulsive
than lions infinity
is the inseparability for the love of particle and void
in a specific field
then the self-energy of the electron takes
the form of an electron exchanging a virtual photograph
the quantum of the electromagnetic folds
the electron with the photograph of the grass with the field itself
with itself fine man owns the field

if the electron shows a self photograph
of itself as a field and then shreds the difficulty
then the photograph goes back
to being itself as a green negative for the love affair
is something immoral
with the infinity of self energy
and related wind infinities
intrinsic
likening is otherwise known as perversion in the field

a pear
touching oneself feeling
or a turning green by oneself faded down
orchard green faded
or touching feeling by oneself faded down
is ambiguity maybe indeterminacy
maybe itself filed down
may itself filed down be immoral
or a violation or a love of fighting moral violations
the very electric essence says not

the very electronic is not mere sea grass
it is sense itself filed down
as we will lemon soon
in a season itself filed down identity
radish wishes
or rather then the very queered dandelions for sure

whether or what is touching feeling oneself faded
the issue is not touching feeling
oneself faded *per se* greening
oneself faded peers see
it is nay rather then the possibility of greening touch
or touching green itself feeling
this issue arises in the field in the fallow way

dandelion gender is not the half of it
then there is the question weather or not what it is
falling over the field

this is this issue arising in the fallow in the following gain

it emits a photograph
it makes a pose sitting down-electron pair
then the pose sitting down and the electron annihilate one another
to make a new photograph
that is ultimate to lately taken inside the electron
inside is absorbing for silverware

if nonfiction gives us such
in fact
an infinite green number
or what fine is fiction man referred to the field
lying beneath the bovine is infinite histories

the electron not only
exchanges a virtual photograph with itself filling
a virtual photograph is still watching action films with itself
it can vanish turning
it is self fulfilling a virtual electron and pose sitting down
then as seen annihilate before returning
to give back a virtual photograph
before it is absorbed by the electron
and so on and so on and so on infinite histories
giving every kind of interaction with every kind
of virtual particle it can interact with
that is there is
a virtual exploration of every infinite set
to awkward dandelions

here is the very green nature of self fulfillment taproot

it is perversity raised dandelions all the way down

every of every kind
that is to say there is as a given
a virtual longing for the love of everything is exploration
it is touching feeling
it is greening feeling
it is a particle greening itself full
it is a particle touching itself filling
and then it is a particle touching green now
and then it is a particle greening touch
and so every level of green
then it is itself fulfillment touched by all other levels of touch
and so on every level of touch
is itself filling out to greet all other levels of green
self-touching is an encounter with infinity of the self full
self-greening is an encounter with infinity
as seen in self fulfillment terrain
matter is an enfolding
an invitation it cannot help touching itself feeling
greeting
and in this self-greening it comes

self touching feeling
is self greening dispersed overhead
is self feeling touching
self greening another dispersed perversity
for the love of the field deeper than we can green on here?

is this perversity obvious
for taproot and unwanted infinity very normalized?

(ghosting to ghost stinging goes
to sting lingering
the sound of the wind in the fog bound trees
the difference between bryn mawr and gladwyne
is that the former means big hill and the latter means
imagined word to sound like glenmede)

expect less to happen
when two different infinities tow willing kind pervasions behind
one is self feeling touching and one is green nakedness
in particular in the singular
there is an infinity to the bear point particle
that it is perverse
that there is only an electron inside a parent thesis
is the undressed dandelion and the bear
outside voice
they separate from the other realization
that it is a systemic cancellation for infinities
an intervention to let infinities cancel themselves
perversion eliminating perversion
cancellation is this
the infinity of the bear point particle cancels
the infinity associated with the could of virtual particles
the bear point particle is the dandelion dressed
by the vacuum contribution
that is the could of virtual particles
the dressed dandelion is thereby realized to be normal
to healed the room rehoused and roof finite
until lambs utilize technical language too
realization is math taming
these infinities that is the infinities get stacked definitively
to give delight
matter to matter in essence gives us
a massive overlaying of perversities seen as infinity infinity

infinity is not only bear or dressed field or undressed dandelions

Misuse

no debt
no doubt to substack
two infinities is in fact a system healed
for the love of a finite value is no small archive
meaning a very sophisticated mathematical machinery needed
to be evolved to make it
none is nevertheless the altitude
for the love of legitimacy
and illegitimacy of real homes
meaning physical chemistry will see the difference
in this sense of that mathematical option
to substack because it does not stick a conceptual cancellation
the infinities can not be avoided
instead run reconnaissance
in the sense to take and count out ten infinities
it is rehoused it is grace it is self field deconstruction
it will continually find ways to open itself filed down
to new possibilities toward iterative reconnaissance figures
ringing then resurfacing overhead
infinities is a sign nodding toward what is vibrant
alive and beside sick

watch the sunrise in the field even if radishes deconstruct
it is only classical ontology and a few keys
it was particles
and the void inside the fountain undone
inside the field the void is not empty
the void is seriously filled determination and indeterminacies

particles are inseparable
from themselves and the void
in particular interacting with the virtual particles of the void and
therefore are inseparable from the void
the plethora is therefore
infinite given the quantum determination seizes on
indetermination seizes as seen in constitutive inclusions

it is a radish doing and undoing its identity
these perversities are intrinsic
these perverse cities are instinct
as soon as pretend it is a city to be reckoned with
or reconnaissance
for desire cannot be eliminated from before
it is being threaded into the unknown insensible

threaded through to overhead?

new indeterminacy and determinacy
it effects matter running around rings it needs to be acknowledged
it needs to be counted done

touching feeling
all greening enters an infinite terrain
soon greening the liminal is touching feeling all lean on
touching feeling the liminal is greening
all lean on
as well as self touching feeling
as well meaning as self greening enters touching
feeling the strings within greening the strings within
matter rests on the unfathomable multitudes
it is an individual all ready will include all possible
intra-actions with itself filed down
and the virtual all
and the non contemporaneous self filed down

every finite gets
threaded through infinite feeling for all other terrains
it is fraught and diffracted
indeterminate agency is doing
and undoing identity it is unsettling foundations
see ride or die identity
to itself filed difference with itself field difference
with itself filed difference
with itself field difference
it is a condition for the self filed distance would
itself field done
to be healed and resist to be indebted
to infinitely many other terrains
here is a debt that does not lie fallow
there is a debt that follows after resisting
and this is a consideration for healing
to ride on green
to ride on touch is to green onto touch
on counting the sense of greening to green
on counting the sense of touching feeling
here is self greening in no way taking away the terrain
that comes to inhabit touching feeling to haunt it
here is self touching feeling in no way taking away the terrain

Julia Rose Lewis

that comes to inhabit the green
at least it specializes green inside touching feeling
it specializes touching feeling inside green

it is only onto logical indeterminacy as a radish
so opens infinite possibilities as matter running rings
that indeterminacy
is infinite openness giving the first condition
for the love affair of all structures
reconnaissance figures in rings stabilities and instabilities
matter in its iterative matter
in its real lizard dynamic is playing
with indeterminate sea and the determined seashore
matter is never a settled matter
it is ready to radish
it cannot be secured and done
the wind conditions with the impossibilities possibilities
and fogged down love affair
and lived indeterminacies are what is the matter with the
shoreline

to gather
do we green when we touch electrons?
do we touch when we green electrons?
hay rather
indecision is cantering and deconstructing
the discussion in the very greening

touching feeling is intra-action
touching feelings
greening is intra-action put into the question
when electrons meet themselves here and halfway in-between
when they green
when they touch then what is being greened in addition
what is being touched?
the varieties will recon figure rings with figure rings
to the shallow ways that electrons get involved in relationships
there is also the fact that matter real lizards itself filed done already
green already touched down
touching feeling in green infinite configuring
touching feeling infinity
intimate touching feelings sensing green sense
hey rather this is matter
matter is conversations of response
and ability touching feeling is a matter of response constituted in
response and ability is constituted in
response and ability to touch green is constituted in
response and ability in green
knits everything

Julia Rose Lewis

together
then foundations for the second edition say
green is never pure or innocent touch
is never pure or innocent green
as such inseparable
the field of differential relations is constituted

touch is infinite
it is green nothingness threaded through
it is a tangible indeterminate day to the heart
matter is not only iterative to lively
it is gregarious intra-actions
it is also infinitely infinitesimally shit through with the terroir
if serious
we see really hard work
when we hear rarely heard work
taking account of constitutive exclusions
then awakening to this infinity of constitutive inclusions
gardens the determinacy and indeterminacy and virtuality at play
it takes a constitutive part
it takes another little piece of finitude to garden a new sensibility

matter rings
it is about the continent temporary
determinate and indeterminate matter and meaning
without fixity
without the fifty cities
without the close shoreline
then the conditions of possibility matter rings
are rings around the the conditions of impossibility
it ties into actions necessary to entail constitutive exclusions
it ties into openness it is important to foot
to take account for phenomena
will necessarily entail taking account of constitutive exclusions
note to take account
for the love affair with the phenomena it is important to foot

Misuse

hew what unfathomable emeralds?
it is a counting task
not only of matter running rings around
it has its own inseparability from the void including the infinite
and abundant nature to bear rabbit inhabitants

there is nonetheless something dripping
even negative
if point is not to widen the bounds to let everything inside

inside is not the same no one human
to gather
to thick cut the inhuman meanwhile
it is intimacy that touches the very green nature
emerald holds
open the space the liveliness of indeterminacies
that bleed through the cuts and inhabit the between entanglements

touching feeling
touching feeling
touching feeling
touching feeling
touching feeling
touching feeling
touching feeling
touching feeling
touching feeling
touching feeling
touching feeling
touching feeling
touching feeling
touching feeling

it takes facing the inhuman within us before touching feeling
to suffering together to feeling moved to have lived

hay rather one then the self filed at the root is response
and ability is not initially filed
instead derived
one can steer reverberations
when response and ability is grass sensibility
in our grass sensibility we get exposed to the outside and bond
exposure is exposure so is the binding vulnerability
to the sensible and outside
if foiling then first outer inner last is sensible inside insensible
outside insensible inside sensible outside

at least touch
at least green negatives list the virtual alive
at the very infinite green indeterminacy and determinacy given
at the heart matter once nothingness
is seen to touch nevertheless
then the infinitude of the void and its indeterminate and
determinate murmuring wall wall ringing out

entanglements get threaded through and dawn inseparable
from the infinite terrain of the virtual lawn

bound to debt
to doubt to indebtedness irreducibly
and materially bound and threaded through the self filed
diffracted and threaded through the self filed dispersed
identity is not coincidence in a file cabinet
no getting away from matter
ringing diffraction
the pattern naturally is not exposed
so ontology values if fiction and if values themselves
radish the world
the very response and ability is not not not

it is hope to hospitality filed down

this is easy as green infinite terrain in touch
with the inhuman
the insensible the irrational the unfathomable and the incalculable
that therefore will help fold deep patterns

whisper over whisper over whisper
for the infinite multitude of indeterminate mess is nonetheless
nay rather it lives and we cannot shit it out
we cannot control it
we cannot leave out the perversity
or the fear revealed in response and ability

to come back
to itself filed done
to diffractively read the murmur
is the background hum human transmitting
to itself filed done neither language nor silence links
nay rather then the encounter rests
it is related to the light light eyes dividing the ground as light

Julia Rose Lewis

inspired down
in this way the wall wallowing murmuring deep patterns is also
alive is also a matter lived outside

it maybe the very touching feeling in many ways green binding
is threaded through
otherwise we might never touch green indeterminacy
and might be touching feeling and feeling green

in discussing the field and wild ideas
I had a muse once upon a time I came across a ghost of my muse
I made fiddlehead ferns in a grey-green kitchen

No Ordinary Work

weld
weed dyer reseda
overdid it
as seen in a biennial light
it is still green and still flowering
if lincoln green
itself found and overjoyed
all the worlds yellow makes with ease
wedded to place like gas station lemonade
and the rustbelt sky beside
weld in the overflow parking lot
at a satellite university
in the sense united it is only a luteolin sun
well in the obsolete sense melted
and woad beside
weld likes to keep itself to itself

woad
the sigh inside
in the obsolete sense tinting
to pigment linen notes
the green nothing of twenty-sixteen
a grey sieve overwinters grass
it is aggressive
it has a south and west aspect
it leaves
it is made into a paste to ferment
it is caked like eyeshadow with sweat
it it left to ferment itself finally
it is infused with lime water after it is pewter blue
as seed-heads
as seen in a biennial likeness
the ocean neolithic continues
nectar rich
this is no ordinary octopus
isatis that is glastum is glass still

madder rose
her red to obsidian berries
it is clinging to circling to invasive
think henna
it could ride that mad hatter
that thoroughbred mare anywhere
in dense racemes
feeds the hummingbird hawk mouth in summer
it is only a stellatarum moon
imagine the hum
waxing
autumn comes to ask
what makes a hawk a hawk?
it likes honeysuckle and woodland edges
as well as the lake color forewings
over to hovering
a migrant with bright clementine hind-wings

alias iris
in the nursery purple
the flower raises florets not petals
if the file is not found
then the water pipe is another canal
only as long as the power lines
and potatoes say they will overwinter
as octopuses say they will
play with dolls
if the spring is following
the alias file is finding bedded dahlias
as a composed head decided dicotyledonous us

Misuse

grace says
some gratuitous octopus
alias dahlias says
also known as cobalt and bulbous
it is royal all the way down
the plum moment
family messenger or rainbow bent
before high performance liquid chromatography
the alum momentum mirrors itself
if the file is not found
then iris is given the inquirer and mirror to read
while the alias file is finding delphinidin glycosides
beside the thickening inks
the octopus is juggling the asparagus spears

Julia Rose Lewis

if the silken birch
as seen in the wood's diagonal light
if and only if the file is right
the pawn finds security
saturn and sliverings of potato tears
raw with a liminal twist
if feather-veined
fun is the salvaged silk taken
if and only if the branch is new fallen
now pioneer zero
is given soaking in a bucket of cold water for a week
the bath water turns to pale ale
if it will be a holiday gift for the shepherd
if and only if the sheep peel leftward
and fold the liminal wooden fence all the way down
it is just deciduous us

walnut lullaby
ashtabula
is not a bad name for a filly
all folded down asleep
her shell is only a hollow ball of cells
a sulking husk
of herself rustling the leaves yesterday
making dye is similar to decommissioning boats
to soak into sinking the old hulls
interest in a stockpot takes a simmer
release and racing and leaping
test its strength
then filter into a glass barn
the dye needs
to run only so many races against itself
to be the color of a black horse at summer end

Julia Rose Lewis

cota tinctoria
it will grow well
it is only a camomile moon
not potatoes not potatoes not potatoes
also known as potassium dichromate
it is snail love
willing life history in stolons
do what you ought to do deadheading
dry heaving
and add the mordant
to be biting to be bidentate
liking the wool fiber ring to be light fast
the jealous yellow as well as golden orange colors
for the love of toxicology not lemons
it is only the bell margin

Misuse

taxus baccata calls
the common needles
no one
deepens the soil
no one
(cares less for taxes
as well as caressing pink ribbons like bark)
the third is not given
beautiful oxen and oxen and car bonnets until
men in decadence until the big hill
paclitaxel is always the answer
the baccalaureate is also known as laurel berry
before the yew wood yields itself to the color rust
trust a triassic fossil to be useful

Julia Rose Lewis

to be beechnuts
velcro is biomimicry
involucre
inner hull lets on leather
grey on green
on vodka on olive green
here colors me alum
beechnuts tartare iron and cotton
to be boiled in the dye pot
to be better roast
soap inside glycoside
foam means
water fat falmouth
it is the long walk back to vermouth
to be bitter
to be rich in toxins tannins tangible
it is bad teeth all the way down
to becoming bark so soft so often carved
fagus sylvatica it is commonly clonal stands

Misuse

hey lady
do you know about bedstraw
sweet gray and sweet woodstuff fair
if filed in a faraway land
tell me everything
stemming from galium verum
vanilla grass and sweet grass
then over rest
soaking over nine hours
pink orange and gin that were given
trick color
then fine as seen in silk
the price of hay grain and raspberry stains
is pastel coral a possible blush?
(also known as aluminum potassium sulfate)
find me a madder rose in the winter time
if it is hard to find
then double gloucester rounds

Julia Rose Lewis

gorse and iron
is a briar-like brain
its arms are only broom making
it is whinchats
in the stead of stone chats and potatoes
as september rent is a sand dump upset
it sends coconut
it sends vanilla all the way
if the soil loans itself yellow portobellos
then everything is given
gorse and iron
and invasive species
and the evergreen horse of course
when gorse is out of bloom kissing is out of season
if the yellow wife is following fashion

gladioli
sepals and petals lie
yellow wishes for sand inside
gloss sides
glass iris similar
gladwyne bryn mawr
it is windows all the way down
always the color will leave the tepals
allow the water to leech
and watch the glad diminutive of sword
swear off the leaves
so gladioli iron citric acid and salt
all washed down and done again
if silk is yellow wishes brown
then yellow wool is willing
then cotton naturally is not overnight pink on gray
light otherwise known as a long flat bone
in a perennial loan
it is windows all the way forward

Julia Rose Lewis

furious eyes
iron no good morning
in purgatory orange
tentative
in an annual light
we see glass animals falling down
like so many cosmos sulphureus
I find myself feeling tan to neon tangerine
to peel a beautiful little
a tongue a stinging organ a knife point
and discover release
fast if a leaf falls into sulking corn
hungry eyes
it is disks and rays all the way down

Misuse

born in the rhubarb family
obtuse if sifting foals sorrels lions
it will soften
nettle stings if found soon enough
then green inflorescences
greet the bitter roan
perianth segments in the outer whorl
are spreading in the inner whorl forming ovate
and wildly triangular fruit valves
from miocene strata
if a leaf is left willing
one on one volume leaves to wool alum
once upon a time to take butter to market
naturally it is not in mint condition

Julia Rose Lewis

genius sorrel
in the buckwheat family
dick dock dick dock
it is cordate bases all the way down
ditches woodland margins and orchards
befitting pink nutmeg ranges
in the dusk sky
it is butter-flowers cooked all the way down
I saw a whale before I saw a man overboard
if a figure eight
if a ferry boat is most beautiful lingering
before the silk wool willing
then figure skating is wicked thickening
as seen in a wooden spoon saucepan and roux mixed

Misuse

cheery
if fortified wine
also known as a palomino
cherry root overnight
iron and power
rate the powder of tartaric acid to take
winner winner crystallized grapes for dinner
overwinter
it is afforestation all the way forward
the winemakers silken circle
bird egg goes begging
cherries and caper-berries and peas oh my!
it is only a stone note
visit traverse city for the definition of winter solstice
is bright or red dark mazzard in deed
is green grey the way the moors blur rain on the window

Julia Rose Lewis

acorns
I take the pain inside
here eye the water and vinegar
rich in iron
how weather rusts
here eye the rich
in bitter sweet tannins
here eye the pigeons rich
in peppercorns
pour over a gray sieve
here eye the rich charcoal linen
it is only potential lasting
twice dyed
also known as wearing the money
here eye the rich indehiscent
here eye the purse singing
dawn is silk tartaric acid alum and a very few acorns

Misuse

cereal leaves
seriously lay me down
low with sore gums mumbling
here is the sugar rushing
she is sorghum husk extracts
in the same subfamily as sugarcane
as I said
it is possible to puff and pop broomcorn
pearl like couscous seeds
I will keep being a husk of myself
this sheath means
seeds and insects inside the little shed house
pink brick brown
it is madder similar all the way down
alum humans grass animals and ethanol always

Julia Rose Lewis

mill left
in a superficial light
it is round and blind to blue gray
like glue
like horseshoe crabs and bears
like iceland and a cherry bakewell tart
she did see the glue in these glue-on horseshoes
naturally it is not a glacier
a glass penis
a pennisetum glaucum comes
wool also willing alum biting to root bound
it is not only scrimshaw pornography and pearls

Misuse

choreography
if figure skating
is a waterbed all the way down
allow wool literal alum
then bedbugs will be afraid
as potatoes see
here are rayed flowers
coreopsis dried in a paper bag
the chorus sings it is tickseed all the way down
if graph writing grin
in the sense written notation for dance
brass to bronze orange
to soda red dresses for the tinctoria sister
if first then drown the dried flower heads overnight

Julia Rose Lewis

if glycerin
is first listening to glucose
it is only letting hands flow to flower
stem to stain
then ethylenediametetraacetic acid
is used to bind iron and shine
it is only miserable blood and water tincture
also known as the weather
lengthening the reins
writing a tangential letter all the way down
the coreopsis sister reads
east in the obsolete sense tinted to west
to ugly bags of mostly water vapor coloring
rising trot
red sky at night riders delight
red sky at morning riders take warning
dear coreopsis does mahogany rhyme with misogyny?

alcea rosea
also known as the ocean in snow
in yellow wine dicotyledons and debt
deepening
bone to bog spavin
even if everything is given in secret
velvet talus
tell us all about tarsocrural longing
is it felting the following wool
is it lightfast
is it rinsing once upon a time a pastel light
recycled shells to shingles to the blueberry door
blue turns into pewter
bloom blossom almost black hollyhocks come back

it is a sin of zinnias
linen needs
to be well left handed
also known as elegant and violent
in the zinnia stem to steam to steed
in winter here legs get the color of sandpaper
they were grown on the international space station
where there is no ornamental lighting
given a lace pattern
given a serpentine registers sessile leaves
it is time to iron out tennessee walker wrinkles
if figure eights all the way down

acanthus
a candle plant
I can not be biting
so often bone does not
turn into a basal rosette yet soap does
in the obsolete sense of lief and love
the silk intoxication is willing
to take iron water and the oyster plant inside
the dye is sea dock and dacquoise sugar rings
the mollis sea holly
is wallpaper all the way down
the petioles longing to be following
water and leaves and breeches over the gray sieve
if and only if it is finishing off snails

Julia Rose Lewis

in a hospital light
a pinecone nevertheless
leaves
a thin needle thrown through the heart
it is stitched down
it needs hot water all the way down
pour over a grey sieve lined with muslin cloth
let rest overnight
let rest overnight
then copper in the obsolete sense arrest
calls for a conference of firs redwoods cedars
and I can neither confirm nor deny
I am finding pinecones
if fossils

Misuse

I wish eucalyptus
well like covered octopuses
petals and sepals lead to a cap
gum mine operculum
come on
come on and take the silk mix
into the soaking color
if winning
then wine fermentation
and a grown migraine
and iron water and tartaric acid and lightning
if foiling the tree first outer inner last
then the bark will survive the fireworks with ease
and eucalyptus beside the new year is only velvet
and shedding and bird nests
and no ordinary ships

Millionth Then

sticks and stones
it wills itself downtown
ticks and cones mark the location
the basin sings to itself
the superb base as basic as baseball love
it is gloves
it is paper flowers all the way down
pits and stones know well
the pastel is less self for the bricks and tissue paper
he is my super wobble blue
also goblin
not to limit the monolith thimble
I think I could do without the rice bedtime maybe
I could and maybe I could not

Julia Rose Lewis

after the stickers
if fish the perennial
leads a low triangular dorsal fin
it is wooden flowers all the way down
he is my super wobble blue
also goblin
peripheral lies the seas
pig go fish as seen in trick house press
as seen in the common the harbor the north
and the north purpose
for the love of porcus piscis
even magic things will come to grief if they fall
against the gray rage and the small toothed whale

Misuse

pins and needles the basin sings
in the stead of dolphins
suddenly it is
bucketing down
it is metal all the way down
as sudden does lie to land in a grey rage
a carrier to convey
I mean the latter sense of a vehicle moving jerkily
he is the outer edge of a waterwheel
otherwise known as the sin cylindrical –
sticks and stones
and the bed depth of a bucket

Julia Rose Lewis

once upon a quiet time
the windmill overlooked the newer cemetery
and the cloud overlooked the windmill
as a featureless sheet
gestures
a middle attitude if stratiform family
he is his chef jacket
the color of the background
as the winds gather a storm to themselves
ahead of the cold or occluded weather
it is quite opaque the cloud that masks me the same

pewter to gossamer
whispers that golden cygnet
is an oxymoron
I mean maybe I could do without the bricks
and stones and maybe I could not
so often the phone screen
has been given to the old diminutive swan
in the cygnet time
sticks and stolen bones will not
walk themselves into the civil twilight

Julia Rose Lewis

if and only
if grey is better
then he is goblin blue
as the cloud overlooks the windmill
before it will swallow the whole fantasy
it is pandemonium
it is tissue paper and flowers all the way down
everyone will pass the swim test
as water returns simple syrup or sugar

Misuse

I know
he may be helium
before variolation in the sense obsolete sea
he may be the way my belly tightens
to say wobbles
maybe I could do without the cloud
and maybe I could not tell
if the porpoise is more blue or masked sky?

Julia Rose Lewis

he is my goblin blue
this minute
the gossamer immunoglobulin
before rice and ribonucleic acid and clouds
maybe I could do without the clear skies
and maybe I could not
satisfy his fantasy of selling the fish

Misuse

if extended
later the gray rage is sugar
running the superb base as baseball love
it gives variolation in the sense obsolete sea
rice and ribosomes
so much for someone else's muse

Julia Rose Lewis

he is my goblin blue
as seas wobble
a simple hydrodynamic model of swimming
watery syrup or sugar
I want him to walk me to the ferry

Misuse

it is only a swan moon
old as the miocene and mean as a phone screen
foraging the greens and the ground nest
see the teeth like needles

Julia Rose Lewis

sticks and stolen bones will not
it is old jokes
it is wooden flowers all the way down

Misuse

as sudden does lie to land in a grey rage
it is whales and snails all the way to the civil twilight

Julia Rose Lewis

I want him here I then will tell him to walk me to the ferry

The Man Trap

mined from Star Trek: The Original Series

Misuse

the ruins ancient
beaming down to the planet
our mission routine
and routine is one woman
past we pick visits
like is like bribing minutes

enter nervous bit
ten years and for all forgotten
all the bone singing
good like a girl a little
less impossible
to follow her routine down
and the intrepid
sense of where to leave salt fact

Julia Rose Lewis

it is different
as grey on gray handsome past
the machine is salt
no no vulcan has no moon
on monitor skin
mooning no reference then
peppers if vessels
of artifacts marked last

on fascinating
this man has no salt thought bones
landing harassing
green find her green leaves hostile
salt salt salt salt salt
salt is green green green green green

Misuse

into green report
as if following nervous
in fact green nipping
green into a minute fact
water or ruins
or concerned your enterprise
as green negative
on fire mine or frighten ten
to engineering
or the last of the salt salt

one continuing
as long as engineering
not dangerous salt
ocean bones salt bones salt bones

Sordes

Misuse

if and only if
sure the pterosauria
sordes pilosus
to go out sorting the glass
so just fault the telescope

Julia Rose Lewis

the glass dinosaur
as if itself found and found
iris is distance
the telescope and the drone
she would spit powdered sugar

Misuse

on telescoping
riven to go out sorting
if in fact the hill
the drone and the inner light
were given this sand castle

Julia Rose Lewis

granularity
in the monastery night
there there disaster
singing into the window
storing droning good morning

Misuse

anaphylactic
as if and only if found
telescope lessons
on and on droning the ghost
seen through the dormer windows

Julia Rose Lewis

as if faraway
was sure a glass pterosaur
was if following
so just fault this telescope
through and through and through and through

Misuse

over and over
this victory of iris
of velocity
to go sort out tomorrow
the telescope and the drone

Julia Rose Lewis

thusly glutinous
glass if and only if found
the lilac cube
glue the glass the glass the glass
in the old brass telescope

exoskeleton
if and only if old glass
is the fictitious
distance between the ocean
the ant and the telescope

Julia Rose Lewis

it is victory
all and only a given
on telescoping
to go out sorting the drone
grey on green on grey on green

www.ingramcontent.com/pod-product-compliance
Lightning Source LLC
Chambersburg PA
CBHW010854090426
42736CB00020B/3454